Images
of
New England

This book features the photography of
James Blank
Shangle Photographics
Charlie Borland

First Printing August, 1992
Published by LTA Publishing Company
Division of Renaissance Publishing Company, Inc.
318 East 7th Street, Auburn, IN 46706

Concept and Design: Robert D. Shangle

Library of Congress Cataloging-in-Publication Data
Images of New England / concept and design, Robert D. Shangle.
    p.   cm.   ISBN 1-55988-216-6 (pbk.): $6.95
1. New England — Pictorial works. I. Shangle, Robert D. II. LTA Publishing Company.
    F5.I45   1992   917.404'43'0222 — dc20   92-27405   CIP

Introduction

"What a beautiful area!" "I want to remember this forever!" "It's absolutely awesome!" "The Creator simply out-did Himself!"

All of these statements are descriptive of the thoughts expressed when viewing this great area of New England, that we live in, work in, and play in. And why not. This is a Grand Place.

Images linger in our mind's eye, bringing back those memories of excitement, happiness, family, loved ones, places we've visited, or always dreamed of visiting. One can remember, either because "I've been there," or visited vicariously. We want to hold onto those experiences of "places I've been, things I've done, places I want to see."

The images in this book have been gathered together to assist with those memories and you can give it life. Combining these pictures with your memories make them fill with energy, telling your story that is full of excitement and thrills.

A tribute to New England!

Portland Head Lighthouse

Rural Vermont

Carrabassett River near Kingfield, Maine

Ashby, Massachusetts

Plymouth Rock Portico, Plymouth, Massachusetts

In the White Mountains, New Hampshire

Old Constitution House, Windsor, Vermont

Mystic Harbor, Connecticut

Rockport, Massachusetts

Bath, New Hampshire

Stonnington, Connecticut

Central Vermont

Acadia National Park, Maine

Ocean Drive, Newport, Rhode Island

Eaton Center, New Hampshire

East Orange, Vermont

Gloucester, Massachusetts

Minute Man statue, Lexington, Massachusetts

Little Lake Sunapee, New Hampshire

Gloucester Coastline, Massachusetts

Harkness Memorial Park, Connecticut

Windsor, Vermont

Bernard, Maine

Old Sturbridge Village, Massachusetts

Portsmouth, New Hampshire

Grand Island

Orrs Island, Maine

Jenny Grist Mill, Plymouth, Massachusetts

New Hope Dam, Hope, Rhode Island

Scituate Reservoir, Rhode Island

Grist Mill at Guildhall Vermont

Sunset at Menemsha, Martha's Vineyard, Massachusetts

New Harbor, Maine

Marlow, New Hampshire

Bass Harbor Head Lighthouse, Maine

Topsham, Vermont

Near Pittsfield, Massachusetts

Wychmere Harbor, Harwich Port, Massachusetts

Prescott Farm, Middletown, Rhode Island

Kent Falls State Park, Connecticut

The Swift River, near Conway, New Hampshire

Mystic, Connecticut

Scituate, Rhode Island

Autumn in White Mountains, New Hampshire

Waits River, Vermont

Gloucester Harbor, Massachusetts

Rangely Lake, Maine

Second Beach, Middletown, Rhode Island